Withdrawn from Stock
Dublin City Public Libraries

D0526549

Stories

Pat Gains

Acknowledgements

The author and publisher would like to thank the headteachers, staff and children of Beverley Manor Nursery School, Nunsthorpe Nursery School, Scartho Nursery School, Elliston Infant School and Strand Infant School for their invaluable help in the production of this book. A special 'thank you' goes to the headteacher and staff of Welhome Infant School for their very kind support in letting the author work with their children on many aspects of this book.

They would also like to give their grateful thanks to Carol Clark for the loan of her story coat and to Anne Perkins for the production of the story box.

The author would also like to thank Ella Burman, Dominic Fell and Harriet Turrell for their kind co-operation in the production of some of the photographs. Thanks are also due to Joan Blandford for the musical ideas and to Karen McCaffery for her patience and artistic flair in displaying the children's work.

© 2000 Belair Publications, on behalf of the author.

Apex Business Centre, Boscombe Road, Dunstable, LU5 4RL.
Email: belair@belair-publications.co.uk

Belair Publications are protected by international copyright laws. All rights are reserved. The copyright of all materials in this publication, except where otherwise stated, remains the property of the publisher and author. No part of this publication may be reproduced, stored in a retrieval system, or transmitted, in any form or by any means, for whatever purpose, without the written permission of Belair Publications.

Pat Gains hereby asserts her moral right to be identified as the author of this work in accordance with the Copyright, Designs and Patents Act 1988.

Editor: Elizabeth Miles
Design: Jane Conway
Photography: Kelvin Freeman
Cover design: Ed Gallagher

Folens would like to thank Frederick Warne & Co. Ltd for allowing reproduction of *Spot* on the front cover.
- *Plum, Peach, Pineapple, Pear* by Mike Jubb from *Food Rhymes* by John Foster and Carol Thompson, published by OUP. Extract reprinted by permission of Mike Jubb.
- *Whatever Next!* © Jill Murphy. Reproduced by permission of Macmillan Children's Books, London.
- *Peace at Last* © Jill Murphy. Reproduced by permission of Macmillan Children's Books, London.
- *Handa's Surprise* © 1994 Eileen Browne. Reproduced by permission of the publisher Walker Books Ltd., London.
- *Elmer* by David McKee, published by Andersen Press, London. Reproduced by permission of Andersen Press, London. Also available from Harper Collins in the USA.
- *Jasper's Beanstalk* by Nick Butterworth and Mick Inkpen, published by Hodder and Stoughton Limited. Reproduced by permission of Hodder and Stoughton Limited.
- *Mrs Mopple's Washing Line* by Anita Hewett, published by Bodley Head. Reproduced by permission of Bodley Head.
- *Mr Gumpy's Outing* by John Burningham, published by Jonathan Cape. Reproduced by permission of Jonathan Cape.
- *We're Going on a Bear Hunt*, text © 1994 Michael Rosen. Illustrations © 1994 Helen Oxenbury. Reproduced by permission of the publisher Walker Books Ltd., London.
- *Where's Spot?* © Eric Hill 1980. The Spot books are published by Frederick Warne & Co., Ltd.
- *My World* by Audrey Curtis and Shelagh Hill, published by Routledge.
- *After the Storm* by Nick Butterworth, published by HarperCollins Publishers.
- *Dear Zoo* © Rod Campbell. Reproduced by permission of Macmillan Children's Books, London.
- *A Dragon in a Wagon* by Lynley Dodd, published by Puffin Books.
- Song from *Okki-tokki-unga*, published by A & C Black.
- *Five Little Leaves*, from *This Little Puffin*, published by Puffin Books/Mallinson Rendel Publishers Ltd.
- *One Day in the Jungle* by Colin West. Published by Walker Books.
- *Walking through the Jungle* by Julie Lancome. Published by Walker Books.

First published in 2000 by Belair Publications.
Reprinted 2003.

Every effort has been made to contact copyright holders of material used in this publication. If any copyright holder has been overlooked, we should be pleased to make any necessary arrangements.

British Library Cataloguing in Publication Data. A catalogue record for this publication is available from the British Library.

ISBN 0 94788 247-2

Contents

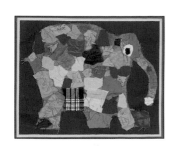

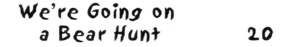

Introduction

The aim of this series is to provide resource material covering all the main areas of young children's learning. Each book is a 64-page full colour resource, designed specifically for educators which provides practical 'hands on' activities suitable for working with the under-fives. They also provide a variety of starting points to encourage and promote creative play.

Written by professionals working in early years education, each book is organised into popular early years themes providing ideas to develop children's linguistic, mathematical, scientific, creative, environmental, and personal and social areas of learning. The key learning intentions are provided for each theme.

Full colour photography offers ideas and inspiration for presenting and developing children's individual work with creative ideas for display. An additional feature of each book is the 'Home Links' section. This provides extension ideas and activities for children to develop at home for each theme.

Most children love listening to stories. A delight in books should be fostered in children from a very early age so that they begin to want to learn to read for themselves. When reading stories, adults can incorporate many interesting and ingenious ways of attracting and maintaining children's attention – they can use their voices in a dramatic way, produce interesting props, such as a story box (a box containing objects from each story, the book and other relevant items) or story coat, or even dress up as a character in the story.

When reading a story:

● always begin by showing the front cover of the book to the children. Ask questions such as: 'What do you think the story is about?' 'What clues are on the cover that tell you this?'

● point out the names of the author and the illustrator, and talk about what authors and illustrators do

● turn the pages slowly, pointing to the words as you read

● talk about the pictures and what is happening in each

● pause at suitable points and ask: 'What do you think will happen next?'

By repeatedly approaching books in this way, children will soon learn that:

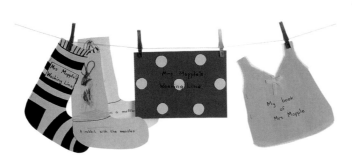

● books in English are read from the front to the back

● an author writes the story and an illustrator draws the pictures

● pages written in English are read from left to right and from top to bottom

● words and pictures carry meaning

● they can predict what will happen next.

But most of all they will learn to enjoy books and want to read them for themselves.

After the Storm

Learning Intentions

- To recall the different roles in the story. To listen carefully and use descriptive language.

- To use positional language correctly. To recognise triangles and squares. To sort and match leaves.

- To know about woodland animals and where they live. To differentiate between natural objects and objects made by people.

- To use leaves for drawing, printing and rubbings. To use a needle to sew around a leaf shape.

Starting Points

- In the autumn take the children for a walk to look at the leaves on the trees changing colour and falling to the ground. Let them walk amongst the leaves and listen to the sounds that the leaves make as they scrunch them beneath their feet.

- On the walk, collect items such as leaves, pine cones, acorns and conkers to make a display in the classroom.

- In the classroom show the children the cover of the book, *After the Storm* by Nick Butterworth. Talk about the title and ask the children: 'What do you think the story is about?' 'What do you think will happen?'

- Read the story and use puppets, soft toys or small plastic models to introduce the woodland animals as they appear in the story. Ensure the children know the names of all the animals, such as the badger, rabbit, fox, mice, hedgehog and squirrel. Ask the children: 'Why were the animals upset?' 'What could Percy do to cheer the animals up?' 'Where else could the animals live?'

Leabharlanna Poiblí Chathair Bhaile Átha Cliath
Dublin City Public Libraries

Language and Literacy

- Change the home corner into Percy's hut. Provide a jacket, hat, Wellington boots, wheelbarrow, brush and armchair. Also, include animal puppets. Encourage the children to play at being Percy and make up their own stories.

- Gather a collection of the different tools that Percy used, introducing their names to the children. Display the children's paintings of Percy's tools in an outline of Percy's wheelbarrow (see Creative Work).

- Encourage listening skills by taping the story and allowing the children to listen to the tape as they follow the story in the book. (When recording, lightly tap a glass with a pencil to indicate a turn of the page.)

- As a group, recall the story and sequence it on large sheets of paper. Encourage the children to recall the names of the animals, the main character and the tools.

- Read and discuss non-fiction texts about different woodland animals. Talk about the difference between story books and information books.

- Make zigzag books of the story. Ask the children to draw the story, putting one picture on each page. They can write their own story using emergent writing, copy writing or by tracing over an adult's writing.

Mathematics

- Use the poster that is supplied with *After the Storm,* if it is available, to count the animals. Use positional language such as 'in', 'on' and 'under'.

- Make sandwiches using jam or lemon curd. Cut them into shapes and name them (square, triangle). Talk about the corners and edges.

- Match leaves that have been collected from outside by the children. Ask the children: 'How shall we sort them'? Sort the leaves into hoops. Count how many are in each hoop.

- Mount individual leaves on card and laminate them. Ask the children to match them by their shape.

- Teach the children 'Five Little Leaves' from *This Little Puffin.*

    Five little leaves so bright and gay
    Were dancing about on the tree one day
    The wind came blowing through the town
    One little leaf came tumbling down.

    (Repeat until none left)

Can you sort these leaves?

- Play 'Kim's Game'. Arrange some woodland animals, a picture of Percy, an acorn and an oak leaf on a tray. Name each of the items and make sure the children look carefully. Cover the tray with a cloth and remove one of the items. Take the cloth away and encourage the children to name the item that has disappeared.

- Introduce the letter 'P', for 'Percy'. Ask the children whose name begins with 'P'. Set up a table with items that begin with 'p'. Each morning name each item, emphasising the 'p' sound. Play 'I Spy'.

Our World

- Make a display of woodland animals. Talk about where they live. Encourage the children to make homes for the creatures from a wide selection of reclaimable materials (include natural materials, such as wood shavings and twigs). Ask the children to paint the homes and display them alongside the animals.

- In the display, include natural objects, such as logs, leaves and acorns, and manufactured objects, such as the tools Percy uses. Talk about the difference between natural objects and those made by people.

- Set the children the task of building a bridge of hollow blocks and large wooden bricks so that others can cross the 'stream' safely. Use a long piece of blue material to represent the stream. Encourage the children to work together to solve the problem.

- Plant acorns and watch them grow over several weeks. Talk about what they need to grow.

Sand and Water

- Hide some acorns, conkers and pine cones in dry sand and have a treasure hunt. Near the sand, place some small trays with number symbols on each one to indicate how many items should go into each. Ask the children to find the treasure and match the items to the number symbol.

- Encourage the children to build bridges and dig burrows and tunnels for the animals in wet sand.

- In the water tray, place boats, play people, plastic woodland animals, pine cones, oak leaves, acorns, branches and materials to enable children to create their own boats. Set the children the task of finding the items that sink and the items that float. Sort them into hoops.

Creative Work

- Paint Percy and any of the woodland animals.

- Let the children draw an oak leaf and an acorn from close observation using a hand lens.

- Encourage the children to paint some of Percy's tools, such as a saw or a hammer. Cut them out and place in an outline of a wheelbarrow.

- Take bark and leaf rubbings. Make a collage or mount them individually and then display them.

- Collect autumn leaves and mount them as a collage.

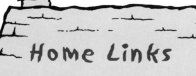

Home Links

Ask parents or carers to:

- collect items beginning with 'p' for a display in school

- collect conkers, acorns and beech nuts and let their children sort them into sets

- complete some bark rubbings with the children, using wax crayons or a candle and paint over the paper

- point out the different-shaped leaves, such as oak, beech and horse-chestnut, during an autumn walk with their children. They could collect the leaves and press them into a book. When they are flat, mount and label them in a photograph album.

- Use hessian and encourage the children to sew using wool in autumn colours. Cut out different-shaped leaves in hessian and let the children sew on them.

- Use the backs of leaves to print. Let the children cut out the prints, then display them attractively (see the photograph on page 1).

- Sew the outline of a leaf. Punch holes into leaf shapes and provide children with large blunt needles and wool for them to make the veins.

  ⚠ Note: Supervise the use of needles.

- Use wool in brown and orange colours to encourage the children to make large pom-poms for the body of a hedgehog.

- Use clay or modelling clay to make woodland animals.

- Play 'The Storm' from Rossini's *William Tell* and ask the children to listen carefully. Ask, 'What does it make you think of?' Encourage them to move like trees blowing in the wind or in a storm.

Whatever Next!

Learning Intentions

● To enjoy stories, memorise their sequence and suggest alternative endings. To engage in different roles.

● To sort and match using three-dimensional shapes. To count forwards and backwards from zero to five or ten as appropriate.

● To design and make models. To use a range of materials to represent objects and places in the story.

Starting Points

● Read the story *Whatever Next!* by Jill Murphy.

● Create a story box containing the book, a small teddy, an owl, a colander, small Wellington boots and some picnic items. Introduce the characters and props.

● Ask adults to act out the story for the children using props.

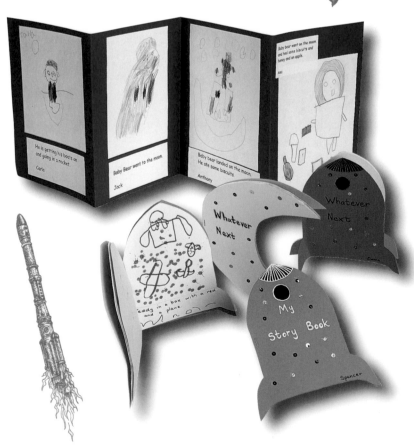

Language and Literacy

● Place the story box in the home corner and encourage the children to use it to act out the story.

● Sequence the story using photocopied or scanned laminated picture cards.

- Play a memory game. Begin with the phrase, 'When I went to the moon I took ...'. Encourage each child to suggest an item. The next child tries to remember and repeat the items that have been said, before adding his or her own.

- Create books about the story. Make them in the shape of the moon or a rocket. Children could draw a picture to represent each part of the story. Adults can write underneath or the children can use their own form of writing.

- Think up different endings to the story. Ask: 'Where might bear want to go next?'

- Point out words in the story that begin with 'b', such as 'bear'. Set up a 'b' table with children bringing things from home to display on it. Every day, use the items to remind children of the sound.

- Make the 'b' letter shape out of sandpaper for the children to trace with their finger as they say the sound. Reinforce this in other areas of the nursery, such as in the sand tray, in small trays of salt and on chalkboards. Use shaving foam to spray on a table-top. Children can practise writing 'b' in the foam.

- Find words or items that rhyme with 'moon'.

- Talk to the children about what they might take in their picnic basket to eat if they went to the moon. In a cut-out basket shape, let them draw what they might take.

- Make the home corner into a space station. Include a computer, a telephone, large boxes covered with silver paper with an array of knobs that can be turned, aerials, antennae, clipboards, and pens for recording details of the flight.

11

Mathematics

- Use the story box display to ask the children to place the bear in different positions. Use appropriate positional language as the bear is moved by asking the children to put the bear 'near', 'under', 'over', 'outside', 'inside', 'beside', 'next to', 'on', 'in', 'above' and 'below' various objects.

- Sort a variety of two- and three-dimensional shapes into sets. Suggest specific criteria, such as 'round shapes that roll' and 'solid shapes that stand flat on the table'.

- Make a block graph showing which food children would take to the moon. Discuss the results.

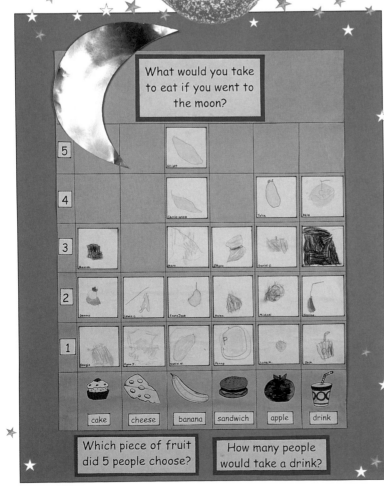

- Make differently sized moon rocks using tin foil. Place a heavy weight in the smallest. Ask the children to estimate which rock will be the heaviest and which will be the lightest. Let them test their theories by first using their hands to weigh the rocks, then using balancing scales to see if they were correct. Use such words as 'big', 'small', 'largest', 'smallest', 'heaviest' and 'lightest'.

- Paint a different number on several paper plates. Ask the children to glue the appropriate number of 'moon rocks' onto the correct paper plate – according to the number symbols on the base of the plate.

- Provide a coloured picture of a rocket in space and encourage the children to match the colours in their own individual pictures.

- Create a wall display to encourage the children to count backwards from 10 to 0 or from 5 to 0.

- Construct a number line from a rod and key tags. Write the numbers 0–5 or 0–10 on it and use when counting forwards and backwards, touching each number in turn. Take turns to cover a number for others to guess which number is hidden. Number ladders can be used in much the same way.

- Teach the children this number rhyme:

  A tall silver rocket
  Is standing on the ground
  Now it's nearly ready
  Here comes the sound
  10, 9, 8, 7, 6, 5, 4, 3, 2, 1,
  Blast off!

Sand and Water

- In wet sand, create a moonscape with rockets, play people, and shapes covered in silver foil. Use it for imaginative play.

Creative Work

● Paint or draw part of the story.

● Make papier-mâché models of the moon's surface from newspaper and reclaimed materials. Use clay to make craters, and fix them onto card with paper strips. Paint these black. Spray the scene with red and orange paint, and add glitter.

● Using a star-shaped cutter and vegetables, print gold and silver stars.

● Add black powder paint and glitter to modelling clay. Press small amounts through colanders, garlic presses and sieves to create the moon's surface on card.

Our World

● Discuss different methods of travelling. Ask the children how they travel to school (by walking, by bus, by car or by bicycle). Ask them about the ways in which they might travel when going on holiday.

● Discuss the differences between the Earth and the moon.

● Ask the children to make a rocket for the bear out of large bricks and hollow blocks. Provide large sheets of paper for them to draw their design. Use large three-dimensional shapes covered in foil to create the surface of the moon.

● Encourage the children to use reclaimed or construction materials to make rockets. Make sandwiches to take to the moon, giving the children a choice of fillings, and cut them into squares or triangles.

Whatever Next!
by
Jill Murphy

Elliott made a rocket at home

'Can I go to the moon?' asked Baby Bear.

We made models of the surface of the moon using 3D shapes

Can you put the moon rocks in the right order?

Which moon rock do you think is the heaviest?

WHOOSH! Out into the night.

- Use black and white paints to make splash paintings on a large piece of paper to represent the sky and stars. Use glitter to enhance the effect. The paintings can be used as a backdrop to display work.

- Listen to the opening soundtrack of *2001 A Space Odyssey* or Holst's *The Planets* suite. Ask the children what it makes them think of. How would they move to the music? If they were going on a trip to the moon, how would they start off – quickly or slowly? How would they move when they were on the moon?

- Use a variety of musical instruments to make the sounds associated with going to the moon.

Home Links

Ask parents or carers to:

- collect items beginning with 'b' and reinforce the letter sound and name at home

- cover the bottom of a baking tray with flour and practise writing the letter 'b' in it

- let their children sort the shopping into shapes that roll and shapes that stand flat

- encourage their children to look at the moon at different times of the month to see how it changes. Find information and pictures about the moon and share these with their children.

Elmer

Learning Intentions

- To recognise and name colours. To empathise with others.

- To recognise and name squares. To sort shapes according to various criteria, such as size and pattern.

- To develop an understanding of two-dimensional maps.

- To develop observational skills and the use of a range of materials to express their ideas.

Starting Points

- Read the story *Elmer* by David McKee, using the story bag to introduce the characters and props.

- Ask the children to describe Elmer's feelings. Use small hand-mirrors so that the children can look at their own faces as they express sadness, joy, anger and fear.

Language and Literacy

- Create a jungle in a corner of the room. Include posters or pictures of jungle animals. Add masks or items of clothing so that the children can role-play these animals.

- Introduce sounds that begin with 'e' in the story, such as 'Elmer' and 'elephant'. Play 'I Spy'.

- Make a sound table and collect items beginning with 'e'. Display and label them. Use the items for playing games, for example, ask children to 'Bring me the egg' or 'Bring me the word that says "egg"'.

- Introduce each of Elmer's colours. Make a large Elmer with each colour as a lift-up flap and ask the children to read the name of each colour underneath the flaps.

Lift the flap to see the colours

- Make small books in the shape of elephants. Encourage the children to decorate the covers and draw pictures from the story inside.

Mathematics

- With the children, count the elephants in the jungle picture as the story is reread. Cut out elephant shapes that will link up to reinforce and record the number of elephants in the story. Encourage individual children to count the elephants and to touch each one as they say the number. (See photograph on page 18.)

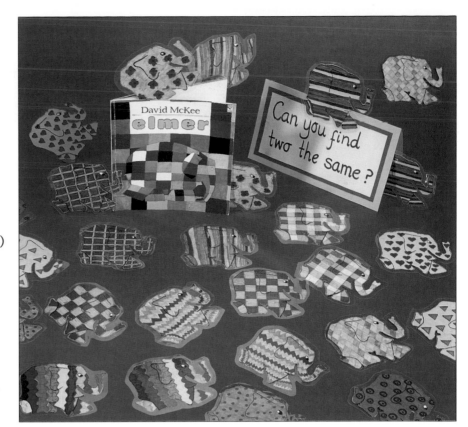

- Introduce squares by pointing out the different coloured squares on Elmer. Provide a selection of two-dimensional shapes and ask the children to find the squares. Gradually introduce triangles and circles. Cut out large shapes and hide them in the jungle corner. Ask the children to find them.

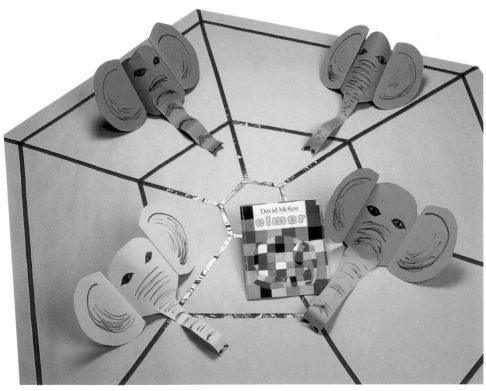

- Make pairs of Elmer cards in different patterns. Ask the children to find the matching pairs. Introduce the words 'pair' and 'different'.

- Make a spider's web on the floor, using sticky tape, and some elephant masks. Introduce the children to the song from *Okki-tokki-unga*:

One elephant went out to play,
Upon a spider's web one day.
He found it such tremendous fun,
That he called for another elephant to come.

One child puts a mask on top of his or her head and walks along the web. Another child is added for each verse. Encourage the children to count the number of elephants before continuing with the next verse and adding another elephant.

- Photocopy three sizes of elephant on to paper. Ask the children to cut them out and glue them onto paper in order of size, from the smallest to the largest. Extend by increasing the number of differently sized elephants.

Our World

- Collect leaves and ivy to make a classroom jungle. Attach leaves to long strips of sticky tape and cardboard rolls. Hang from the ceiling or against a wall.

- Talk about what it would be like in a jungle. Work together to create a jungle in the brick area. Make paths with sand, water holes out of blue paper and trees with greenery collected from the garden. Draw a map of your classroom jungle.

- Make patterns by decorating squared biscuits with icing, pieces of fruit and glacé cherries. Use red, blue and yellow food colouring and drop a small amount of colour on to the icing.

- Let the children experiment with coloured, sugar-coated sweets. Either let them suck the sweets and look at the sweet now and again or add a few drops of water to a sweet on a saucer. How do the sweets change? Ask them what has happened to the colour. Do they know why it has disappeared?

- Repeat the experiment by adding drops of water to other types of sweets. Does a similar thing happen?

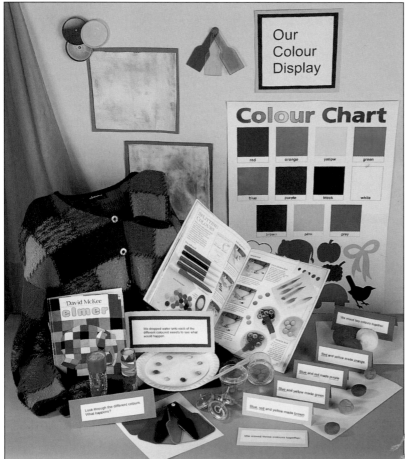

- Explore what happens when small amounts of red and yellow dough are rolled together. Repeat with red and blue, and then blue and yellow dough. Continue the colour experiment with the three colours.

- Drip blue and yellow paint onto white material and encourage the children to describe what they see as the colours mix.

- Use red, blue and yellow powder paint. Encourage the children to mix two colours together and observe the result.

- Create a colour display with examples of the above experiments, labelling each one.

Sand and Water

● Place different strips of coloured crêpe paper in the water tray. Encourage the children to observe how the strips change in water.

● In dry sand, create a jungle scene with a water hole, logs, greenery and jungle animals and use it for imaginative play.

● Provide small trays of flour or salt for the children to make patterns with their fingers.

Creative Work

● Draw, paint or print leaves for a jungle scene. Cut them out when dry and display them in a jungle corner. Then draw and paint pictures of jungle animals and add them to the picture.

● Make an Elmer. Provide a selection of different materials for the children to choose from to cut into squares and stick or sew on to Elmer.

● Learn colour songs, such as 'Sing a Rainbow' from *Apusskidu*, and poems about colours. Colour poems can be found in *Hailstones and Halibut Bones* by Mary O'Neill.

● Make sound patterns using musical instruments. Use sticks to make patterns to 'ha-ppy' and 'sad'. Children can copy the patterns by clapping.

Home Links

Ask parents or carers to:

● help the children look for patterns in the home, such as on floor tiles, in windows or on wallpaper, and to use wax crayons to take rubbings of the patterns

● let the children look for pairs of gloves and socks that are the same or different

● let the children count and sort sweets into groups of different colours.

We're Going on a Bear Hunt

Learning Intentions

- To recognise patterns in sounds, distinguishing between individual sounds and letters.

- To enjoy the repetition in a story, while listening and repeating familiar phrases.

- To place items in sets using different criteria, and recording in a variety of ways. To use non-standard measures and to compare sizes.

- To know that water evaporates in heat, turns to a solid when frozen, and then returns to its liquid state when warmed.

- To use a variety of materials to represent characters in the story.

Starting Points

- Ask the children to bring a teddy bear to school. While sitting in a circle, allow each child to tell the person sitting alongside them about their bear. Each child can later tell the whole group about the bear. If encouragement is needed, ask about the colour of the bear, its name and its size.

- Read the story *We're Going on a Bear Hunt*, by Michael Rosen and Helen Oxenbury.

- Make an attractive display in the classroom of the children's bears.

Language and Literacy

- Make a story box to hold the book, and add puppets for each of the characters as they are made (see Creative Work, page 25). Encourage the children to act out the story using the children's own puppets.

- Read the story once more, showing and discussing the pictures with the children. Pause after each line for the children to repeat it, encouraging them to do the actions to 'over', 'under' and 'through'.

- Point out the capital letters in 'WHAT'S THAT?' and 'IT'S A BEAR'. Ask why these sentences are in capital letters. Accept all their answers before explaining that they need to say these sentences in a very loud voice.

- Ask the children to predict how long the bear hunt took and what they think the bear will do next. How did he feel?

- Talk about different possible endings to the story. Ask the children to draw these and, in their writing, write their own ending to the story.

- When reading the story again, ask the children to listen to the difference between 'swishy', 'swashy'; 'splash', 'splosh'; 'squelch', 'squerch'; 'hoooo', 'woooo'. Make labels and encourage the children to look closely at the words and see if they can point to the letter that is different in each pair.

- Set up a cave in the home corner so the children can use it for their own story of the 'Bear Hunt'.

Mathematics

- Count the number of brown bears, cream bears and white bears, etc. Ask the children to draw their bear on a circle of paper and make a block graph. Explain how to 'read' the chart. Ask questions, such as: 'How many white bears are there?'

- In a small group, ask the children to predict which is the heaviest and which is the lightest bear. Use a bucket balance to check their predictions, recording the findings.

- Place one of the bears on the table and ask the children to predict how many multilink cubes it will take to measure from the bear's toes to the top of its head. Test the results. Repeat using a differently sized bear. Ask: 'Which is the tallest?' 'Which is the shortest?'

- Use a box to represent a cave and ask individual children to put their bear in different positions, for example 'behind', 'in front of', 'beside', 'in', 'over' and 'under'.

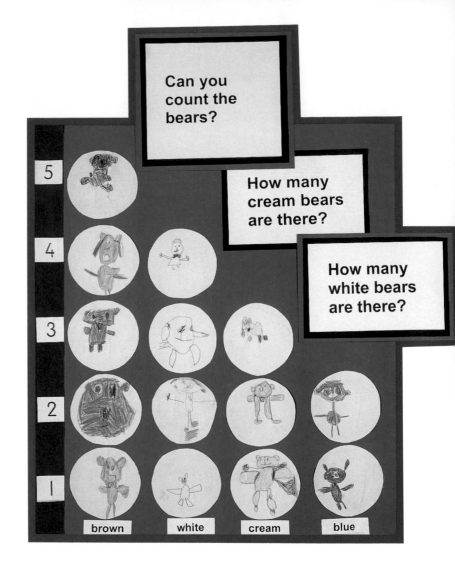

Can you count the bears?

How many cream bears are there?

How many white bears are there?

5 4 3 2 1

brown   white   cream   blue

- Look at the display collection of bears and ask the children to decide on one thing that they could make a set of, for example bears with a bow, large bears, brown bears. Repeat until all the bears have been placed in sets.

A set of brown bears

A set of 'not brown' bears

- Provide a set of coloured bears and ask the children to place the yellow bear first, the blue bear second and the red bear third. Make labels: 1st, 2nd and 3rd.

- Compare the sizes of adults' and children's footprints.

22

Ordering from the smallest to the largest

- Gather a selection of five bears and ask the children to place them in order, with the largest first and the smallest last. Record the results. Then repeat the ordering but with the smallest first and the largest last.

- Make an obstacle course to represent the 'Bear Hunt' so that children can go 'through', 'over', 'up', 'down', 'under', etc. as they follow the path taken by the characters in the story.

- Make a board game to represent the 'Bear Hunt'. Shake a die and move a play person the appropriate number of squares.

- Make a 'bear game'. Provide a card with an outline of a bear for each player. Cut up duplicate bear shapes into six parts (two legs, two arms, a head and a body). Label all the parts with a number and matching number of dots. The same labels should be put in matching positions on the outlines. Throw a die and match the appropriate body part to cover the bear outline. Continue until all the children have completed a bear.

Our World

- Use differently sized shoes and paint their bases with water. Print them on the outside playground and watch the water evaporate. Encourage the children to describe what is happening.

- Encourage the children to make a vehicle that is just the right size for their own bear to escape from the cave. Provide a range of materials, including reclaimed materials, construction pieces, small and large bricks. Encourage them to evaluate their vehicle. How could they improve it?

- Sow grass seeds in a large seed tray. Once it has grown use it, along with play people, to recreate part of the story. Discuss what grass seeds need to make them grow.

Sand and Water

- In the water tray, add soil or compost to make mud. Let the children explore the texture. Write and display the words that the children use to describe it.

- Freeze water in a variety of containers, such as yoghurt pots, margarine tubs and a large balloon. Remove the ice shapes from the containers and place in the empty water tray. Encourage the children to watch as the ice melts and changes shape.

- Create a forest in wet sand, using greenery that the children have collected and adding sticks and stones. Use it for imaginative play, recreating the journey through the forest.

We're going on a bear hunt

Creative Work

- Make puppets of the characters in the story. Use paper bags filled with screwed-up newspaper, cardboard or paper plates on sticks.

- Make prints in clay using different sizes and patterns of the soles of shoes.

- Make a cave out of a large cardboard box. Attach crumpled pieces of newspaper and pieces of polystyrene to the box and cover it with black paint, crêpe and tissue paper. Arrange greenery and ferns around it. Place a large bear inside, as if it is hiding, and use it for imaginative play.

- Use vegetables to print the bear's footprints.

- Paint the characters in the story.

- Add powder paint to dry sand. Encourage the children to dribble glue on the surface of a piece of paper and shake the sand mixture onto it to make patterns.

- Use musical instruments, and the voice and the body to accompany the story. Make a tape of the end result.

Home Links

- Send a special bear home with a different child each night with a letter saying:

  Hello,
  I am Bertie Bear.
  Please look after me. I would like to do lots of things at your house.
  Love, Bertie.

Ask parents or carers to:

- return the bear to school the next day so that their child can tell everyone what the bear did when it was at his or her house

- make sure that a teddy is brought to school for the display

- point out capital letters on signs such as 'STOP', 'EXIT'.

Dear Zoo

Learning Intentions

- To develop listening, imaginative and talking skills. To recognise letters by shape and sound and to write letters and words.

- To develop pattern-making skills. To match and recognise numbers. To develop the use of mathematical language, such as 'long', 'tall', 'bigger' and 'smaller'.

- To develop an awareness of the world. To explore and recognise features of living things by looking at patterns and differences. To use materials to develop skills such as cutting, folding and building.

- To develop the imagination through sound, texture, language, shapes and space.

Starting Points

- Make a story coat by adding felt pockets to a jacket. Decorate the coat with braid, sequins, buttons and badges. Use the pockets to hold the animals from the story. As the story is read, an animal can be produced from the pocket it is hiding in.

- Set up a display of books, pictures and words about wild animals. Ask the children if they know the names of any wild animals. Name some of the animals: elephant, lion, giraffe, and show a picture of each animal as you talk about it.

- Show the children the cover of the book *Dear Zoo* by Rod Campbell. Read them the story. Ask the children to predict which animal might be in each of the boxes sent by the zoo.

Language and Literacy

- Name and display all the animals and write a label on a strong parcel tag for each one. Ask the children to match the tags to the animals. (Draw a picture of the animal on the back of each tag for the children to self-check.)

- As the children are introduced to each animal in the story, say the initial letter of the animal's name, for example 'l', 'm', 's' and 'p'. Provide pictures of lions, snakes, monkeys and puppies and ask the children to sort them according to their initial sound.

- Encourage the children to retell the story using puppets. Make the puppets available in the imaginative play area for the children to use.

- Make zigzag books with 'Dear Zoo' on the cover, and write 'So they sent me a ...' on each page. Children draw what they were sent and can be encouraged to write using their own symbols or letters.

- Set up a writing box or table with paper, envelopes, postcards and tags labelled 'From the Zoo', and a postbox. Ask the children to write a letter to the zoo.

- Encourage children to make up their own stories about a trip to the zoo. Draw simple pictures on card and laminate them. Let the children put the cards in the correct order to tell the story of a trip to the zoo.

- Discuss what the animals look like. Are they fierce, grumpy, happy or sad? Provide the children with small mirrors and let them make animal faces to match.

- Introduce capital letters and encourage the children to find 'DANGER', and 'FROM THE ZOO' in the story. Point out the capital letters in their own names.

Mathematics

- Use material and prints similar to the markings and fur on tigers, zebras and leopards. Let the children compare and match the pattern to the animal.

- Make a game using a cloth-covered board, pictures of animals and numbers on cards. Ask the children to match the number symbols to the number of animals.

- Use toy animals to count how many different animals were sent to the zoo.

- Cut pictures of animal heads in half then use mirrors to see the complete heads. Ask the children which are symmetrical and which are not symmetrical, emphasising and explaining the new vocabulary.

- Provide differently sized animal pictures for the children to cut out. Ask them to place them in order of size, from the smallest to the largest. Make individual books with the results, entitled 'My book of sizes'.

- Make a board game using a large die with a picture of an animal on each side. Ask the children to match the animal.

- Encourage the children to learn this number rhyme:

  1, 2, go to the zoo
  3, 4, leopards roar
  5, 6, chimp's tricks
  7, 8, penguins wait
  9, 10, lion's den.

- Provide a range of differently sized boxes. Give the children a selection of different animals and ask them to predict which animal will fit into each box. Let them test their predictions.

- Let the children draw around their hands and cut out several copies. Ask them to measure the length or height of toy animals from the story. Make a class book of the results, for example: 'The giraffe is ... hands tall', 'The lion is ... hands long'.

Which animal fits into the box?

Sand and Water

- In the dry sand tray, create a zoo for animals by making enclosures with small bricks. Use it for language development and role play.

- Create a swamp in the water tray, with snakes, crocodiles, logs and greenery and use it as above.

Our World

- Show a globe to the children and discuss which place they think each animal comes from – hot areas or cold areas? Point to your country and then to places such as Africa, where many animals, including lions, giraffes and elephants, live.

- Discuss the various features of the animals. For example, ask why camels have large feet and a hump; why giraffes have long necks; why lions are a golden colour, and why snakes slither along the ground. Talk about camouflage.

- Let the children construct cages for different animals from reclaimed materials. Cover the cages or boxes with paper.

- Use play mats and miniature zoo animals to create a zoo on the carpet.

Creative Work

- Use a variety of paints (finger paint, tempera blocks, powder paint and ready-mixed paint) to paint different animals from the story.

- Provide a selection of collage materials suitable for making animal pictures. Children can feel as well as look before deciding which material would be best for their chosen animal.

- Encourage the children to model animals from clay, modelling clay, salt dough or papier mâché.

- Provide a variety of materials for the children to make masks of animals to use in role-play.

- Use plain socks to make animal hand puppets. Sew or stick on felt pieces, beads, buttons and sequins for the appropriate features.

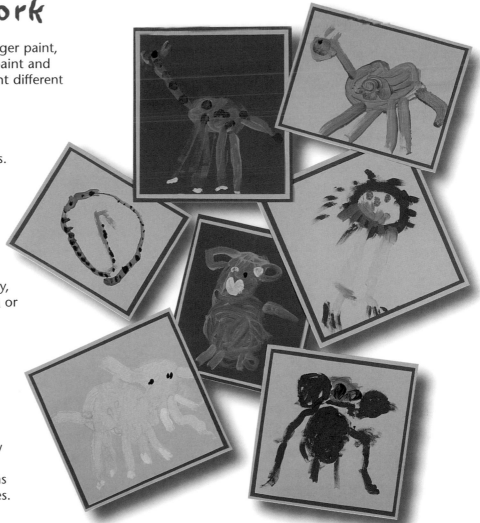

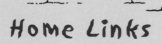

Home Links

Ask parents or carers to:

- take their children to the zoo or a safari park, if possible

- watch nature programmes on television for a short time with their children

- listen with their children to a tape of an animal book that the teacher will supply.

- Set up a zoo or a shop with soft toy animals. Ask the children what should be in it and try to incorporate their suggestions. Let the children use the display for role-play.

- Play excerpts of music from *Carnival of the Animals* by Saint-Saëns. Encourage the children to move to the music as if they were the relevant animal.

- Teach the children the words to 'Old Macdonald' but change the words to say he 'had a zoo'. Let the children suggest the sounds the animals might make.

- Teach the children the song, 'Daddy's Taking Us to the Zoo Tomorrow' from *Apusskidu*. Encourage the children to join in the actions to the song by: swinging an arm for 'long, trunk swinging'; scratching their sides for 'scritch, scritch, scratchin'; and sighing heavily for 'huff, puff, puffing'. Let the children select an instrument for each verse to accompany the singing.

Handa's Surprise

Learning Intentions

- To encourage children to listen carefully and identify initial sounds through listening and observation.

- To give children practical experience of early addition and subtraction.

- To know about different types of fruit and where they grow. To use a simple plan of the room.

- To paint, draw and model items in the story.

Starting Points

- Read *Handa's Surprise* by Eileen Browne. If possible, put the fruits mentioned in the story in a basket to introduce to the children. Emphasise the names of the fruit (banana, guava, orange, mango, pineapple, avocado, passion fruit and tangerine) as you show them.

- Place toy animals in the pockets of the story coat (see page 26) and introduce each one as they eat a fruit in the story. Make sure the children know the names of the animals and birds (monkey, ostrich, zebra, elephant, giraffe, antelope, parrot and goat).

Language and Literacy

- Set up a fruit and vegetable shop. Children should take turns to be the customers and the shopkeeper. Make sure there are notices for the children to read and include a telephone, directory, cash register and times of opening. Supply blank shopping lists for children to fill in as they use the shop.

- Introduce the children to common fruits such as oranges, apples, pears, bananas, grapefruit, melons, grapes and lemons. Ask them to name them and describe their shape, colour and smell.

- Let the children talk to their friends about their favourite fruit. Encourage them to draw their favourite fruit and an adult can write a sentence: 'I like ... because ...'. Display the drawings and encourage the children to read about each other's favourite fruit.

- Make a display of the children's paintings and label them, emphasising the initial sound in the names of the fruit. Ask the children to find two fruits with the same initial letter and sound. Then encourage them to match the sounds to the initial letters of the fruit.

- Display and label the animals from the story. Ask the children to listen to the initial sound in the names of the animals. Then encourage them to find the name of the fruit and the name of the animal that begins with 'm'. Repeat with 'g', 'o', 'p' and 'a'.

- Sketch the events in the story onto cards. Ask the children to sequence the story by putting the cards in the correct order.

- Play the game 'I went to the shop and I bought a ...'. Children repeat what the other children have said and add their own item, using props to help them remember. Make shopping lists by drawing the fruits they would like to buy from the shop.

- Place one or two distinctive fruits in a bag. Ask the children to feel inside the bag and describe a fruit without saying its name, so that the other children can identify it.

- Make a list of 'Tastes I like' and 'Tastes I dislike'. Encourage the children to draw pictures to illustrate the list.

- Teach the children this poem:

Plum, peach, pineapple, pear
I could eat you anywhere.

Pear, plum, pineapple, peach,
Come for a picnic on the beach.

Peach, pear, pineapple, plum,
Hurry up and give me some.

Mike Jubb

33

Mathematics

- Sort the fruit into sets, for example bananas/not bananas. Make sets of 4 oranges, 3 tangerines and so on, and record the results.

- Use the fruit in the basket to subtract one each time an animal takes it away. Say to the children: '7 take away 1 leaves 6', etc. Then replace the fruit one by one and add one each time: '0 add 1 makes 1'.

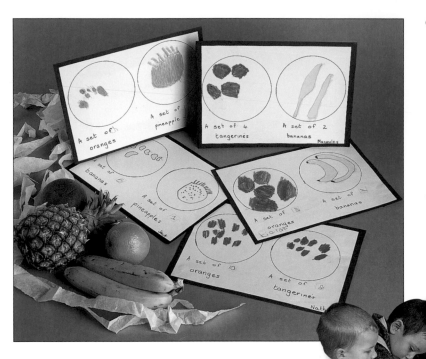

- Place price tickets on the fruit and vegetables in the classroom shop. Encourage the children to buy the fruit using real or play money and the correct coins. On a sheet of card mark out the correct number of spaces for the different coins. At the end of the day, nominate a shopkeeper to check that no coins are missing.

- Weigh the fruit using construction cubes to find which are the heaviest and lightest. Draw the results.

Sand and Water

- Place a selection of fruits near the water tray. Ask the children to guess which fruits will float and which will sink. Let them test out their predictions. Supply two hoops for sorting the fruit into two groups: fruits that float/fruits that sink.

- In the wet sand tray set up 'Handa's journey'. Make Akeyo's hut, use greenery for the trees, and make paths through the corn and grass. Include the animals hiding amongst the trees. Use it for imaginative play.

Our World

- Visit a fruit and vegetable shop. Photograph the visit and use the pictures to make a reading book with simple sentences under each photograph.

34

- Let the children feel and smell a selection of different fruits. Can they name the fruit? What colour is it? What shape is it? Is it juicy? Do we peel it before we eat it? Does it have pips or seeds? Cut the fruit in half and show the inside of the fruit. Use a magnifying glass to look more closely. Cut off a small piece for the children to taste. Discuss what the fruits taste like and which one they like best.

- As the fruit is cut, point out the seeds. Plant some and watch them grow.

Home Links

Ask parents or carers to:

- take their children with them when they go shopping. At the fruit counter, they should look at the different types of fruit and name them. If possible, they could buy an unusual one, encouraging their child to feel, smell, describe and then taste a piece of it.

- collect 7 items, and encourage their children to take one away, saying '7 take away 1 leaves 6', etc. each time until there are none left. Then add one each time, saying '0 add 1 is 1', etc.

- Discuss which country the fruit comes from. Ask: 'Does it grow here or in a hot country?' On a world map or globe, point out the countries where the fruit might grow. Talk about Kenya, where the story is set.

- Set out the room for children to go on a journey to numbered cones in different areas of the classroom. Introduce a simple plan of the classroom with the cones clearly marked. Children can take a ticket with a picture representing the area (for example, the home corner) and a number on it, and find the route to the correct cone. They can then play with the items in the chosen area.

Creative Work

- Use chalks or pastels to draw the fruit and use the pictures in a display in the shop area.

- Make salt dough and use it to model the fruit. Dry out in a slow oven to harden and paint with appropriate colours. Use the fruit in the classroom shop (see photograph above).

- Make prints using half oranges or lemons.

Mr Gumpy's Outing

Learning Intentions

- To learn new vocabulary, for example 'bleated' and 'squabbled'. To recall the sequence of the story.

- To develop sorting and counting skills.

- To recognise and name farm animals. To develop an understanding of floating and sinking.

- To become familiar with different types of painting. To choose different materials to create different textures.

Starting Points

- Read the story *Mr Gumpy's Outing* by John Burningham to the children, introducing each of the characters in turn and taking them out of the prop box.

- Adults could act out the role of Mr Gumpy and the animals. If there is only one adult available, invite the children to join him or her to be the other characters in the story. Use a piece of blue material for the river and building blocks or a large cardboard box for the boat. Add other props such as a hat and pole for Mr Gumpy.

Language and Literacy

- Sketch the events in the story onto cards. Use a cloth-covered board for children to sequence the events in the story.

- Prepare a card with rows of animals. In each row include one that is different to the rest. Ask the children to find the odd one out. Ask them why it is different.

- Make a book of the story in the shape of a boat (see photograph on page 36). Use one page for each animal that joins the boat. Encourage the children to make up their own story and read it.

- Prepare cards for a matching game. Draw items associated with each animal or person, for example a bone for the dog, a ball of wool for a sheep, a feather for a hen.

- Encourage the children to look closely at an animal in the story and describe it to the child next to them. Can they guess which animal it is?

- Play sound lotto. Cover boards with pictures of animals in the story and make a tape of the sounds that the animals make. Children play the game by covering up a picture on the board each time they hear the sound of the animal.

- Set up a display of the characters in the story and label them. Ask the children to bring items to you, for example the goat. Extend this by asking them to bring you the writing that says 'the goat'. Let them match the word to the object.

- Introduce the letter 'g' and the sound it makes. Ask the children to find words beginning with 'g' in the story ('Gumpy', 'goat', 'goodbye'). Play 'I Spy'. Set up a display of items beginning with 'g'. Label them.

- Encourage the children to act out the story, using large hollow blocks for Mr Gumpy's boat and long pieces of blue material to represent the river. Provide a hat, jacket and Wellington boots for Mr Gumpy, and masks for the animals. Use for role-play.

Mathematics

- Make a strip book of the story of Mr Gumpy. Ask the children to draw pictures of characters in the story and add them, one by one, to the book. Let the children use them to count the number of characters in the story.

- Set toys representing the story's animals and children on a table, for the children to count. Ask: 'How many will there be if the rabbit jumps into the river?' 'How many will there be if the goat gets off the boat?' Give the children lots of practical experience of taking 1 away.

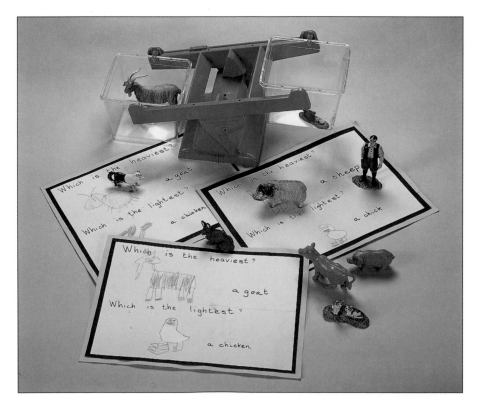

- Introduce ordinal numbers by using such phrases as 'the children first', 'the rabbit second'. Children can place the characters in the order in which they climb into the boat with labels saying 1st, 2nd, etc.

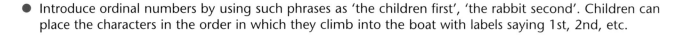

- Estimate which toy animal is the heaviest and which is the lightest. Weigh them using balancing scales and label them 'heavy' or 'light'. Ask the children to record the results by drawing the animals. Find the toys that balance on the weighing scales.

- Provide a selection of each type of animal from the story and sort them into sets, such as sheep or cows. The children can count them and find the correct numeral.

38

Sand and Water

- In the water tray put boats or rafts containing small animals and play people. Place Mr Gumpy in his boat with the animals from the story around the edge of the tray. Encourage the children to use the models to act out the story.

- Place a selection of different coloured boats in the water tray. Attach a sticky-backed hook to each boat. Let the children use rods with a curtain hook attached to a piece of string to hook a boat out of the water. Ask them to sort the boats by colour.

- Set up a tray or bowl of water and gather together a selection of natural and manufactured objects, including some toy animals from the story. Let the children predict which will float and which will sink, before testing out their predictions. Ask the children to sort them into two groups, saying 'These float' and 'These sink'.

Our World

- Using families of animals, find the baby of each type and name them. For example, ask: 'What is the baby cow called?' Make sure that they know the names (cow, calf; sheep, lamb; goat, kid; cat, kitten; dog, puppy; pig, piglet; hen, chick; rabbit, kitten). Label them.

- In a building merchant's tray, set up a river and boat scene to represent Mr Gumpy and the fields in which the animals live. Encourage the children to use it for imaginative play.

- Let children make some of the items that Mr Gumpy had for tea, such as jelly and sandwiches. Give them a choice of sandwich fillings and colours for the jelly and take them shopping to buy what is needed. Have a tea party like the one in the story.

Creative Work

- Encourage the children to make boats from reclaimed materials. Paint them and use in a large display.

- Encourage the children to use a range of materials, such as pencils, felt-tipped pens, charcoal, chalks, crayons and pen and ink to draw Mr Gumpy and the animals.

- Use malleable materials, such as clay or dough, to make models of the characters in the story. Use feathers, pipe-cleaners, matchsticks and small stones to add to the clay models before they dry. When dry, paint and varnish the models.

- Encourage the children shape their favourite food for a tea party out of salt dough and to paint it. These items can be used in a role-play area, set up as Mr Gumpy's house.

- Mix equal amounts of blue paint and washing-up liquid in a margarine pot, fill with water and stir well. Let the children blow into the mixture through a straw and take prints of the bubbles by pressing paper lightly on top of the pot. Cut into triangular and circular shapes, mount and use as the river when displaying work on *Mr Gumpy's Outing*.

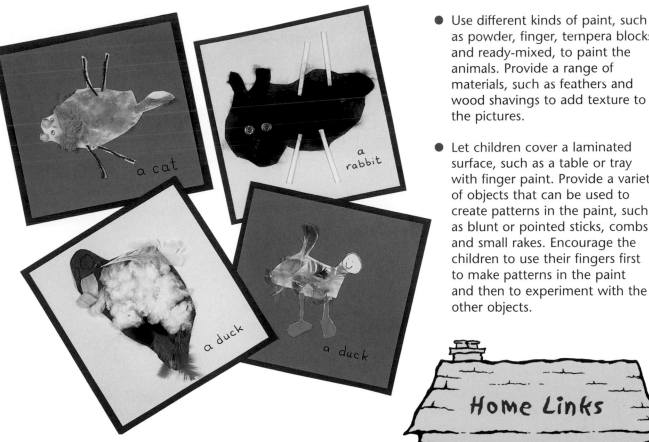

a cat

a rabbit

a duck

a duck

● Use different kinds of paint, such as powder, finger, tempera blocks and ready-mixed, to paint the animals. Provide a range of materials, such as feathers and wood shavings to add texture to the pictures.

● Let children cover a laminated surface, such as a table or tray with finger paint. Provide a variety of objects that can be used to create patterns in the paint, such as blunt or pointed sticks, combs and small rakes. Encourage the children to use their fingers first to make patterns in the paint and then to experiment with the other objects.

Press a piece of paper onto completed patterns and leave to dry. These can be used in a large display.

● Set up a woodwork bench and provide a selection of different sized pieces of wood, and child-safe tools such as a hammer, nails and some sandpaper. Encourage the children to make a boat for Mr Gumpy.

⚠ Note: Ensure that children are supervised throughout this activity.

● Provide pictures and toy animals from the story and a selection of materials, such as paper bags, boxes, card, paper, foil, transparent plastic, feathers, wood shavings and paper plates and dishes. Encourage the children to make three-dimensional models of the animals.

● Set up a 'sound table' with a variety of instruments that can be blown, banged, scraped, plucked or shaken. Include materials that make different sounds, such as coconut shells, keys, large nails, pieces of wood, pottery flowerpots and sandpaper blocks. Children can make their own instruments, for example, shakers can be made from clear sealed tins of rice, peas or sand. Introduce only a few instruments to the group at one time. Tell the children what they are called and how to use them correctly. Change the instruments regularly.

● Teach the children the words to 'Down By the River the Green Grass Grows' from *Musical Starting Points with Young Children*. Let the children choose an instrument from the sound table to accompany the tune.

Home Links

Ask parents or carers to:

● reinforce the name of the letter 'g' and the sound it makes. Collect items beginning with 'g' for display in school

● put items in the bath so that children can predict which will float and which will sink

● let their children set the table for a meal, matching one to one

● take their children on a visit to a farm

● save a large cardboard box for their children to use as a boat. Dress up as Mr Gumpy with old clothes and encourage them to retell the story or make up their own.

Where's Spot?

Learning Intentions

- To recognise repeated phrases. To sequence the story, act it out and use the language in the book.

- To know and understand positional language. To count and match items to numerals correctly.

- To select appropriate materials to make models and use skills such as cutting and joining.

- To respond to the story using a range of materials and forms of expression – through puppets, paintings, drawings and models.

Starting Points

- Read the story *Where's Spot?* by Eric Hill. Use the story bag to introduce the characters from the story.

Language and Literacy

- Sketch the events in the story onto cards. Place them on a cloth-covered board and encourage the children to sequence the story by putting the cards in the correct order.

● In the home corner, arrange a bed, a rug, a basket and some large cardboard boxes painted to represent a grandfather clock and wardrobe for the children to hide in. Have notices around the home corner, such as: 'Is he inside the clock?' 'Is he under the bed?' 'Is he in the wardrobe?' Encourage the children to use these for imaginative play and for re-enacting the story while repeating the phrases in the book.

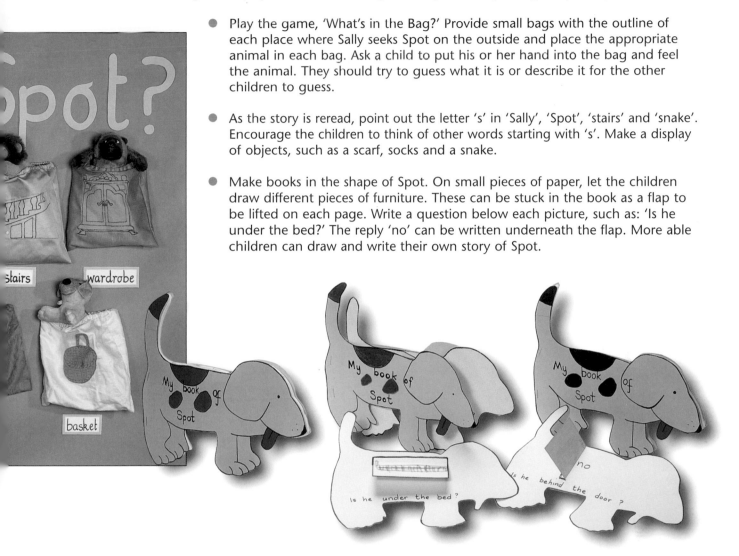

● Play the game, 'What's in the Bag?' Provide small bags with the outline of each place where Sally seeks Spot on the outside and place the appropriate animal in each bag. Ask a child to put his or her hand into the bag and feel the animal. They should try to guess what it is or describe it for the other children to guess.

● As the story is reread, point out the letter 's' in 'Sally', 'Spot', 'stairs' and 'snake'. Encourage the children to think of other words starting with 's'. Make a display of objects, such as a scarf, socks and a snake.

● Make books in the shape of Spot. On small pieces of paper, let the children draw different pieces of furniture. These can be stuck in the book as a flap to be lifted on each page. Write a question below each picture, such as: 'Is he under the bed?' The reply 'no' can be written underneath the flap. More able children can draw and write their own story of Spot.

● Play 'Kim's Game' by placing the objects from the story on a tray or table. Name each item, asking the children to repeat its name. Cover with a cloth and secretly remove one item. Uncover the tray and ask the children to name the item that has been removed.

● Use puppets to retell the story, letting different children be different animals.

● Make a simple lotto game with the animals in the story. An adult names the animals before showing the picture to the children. The child with the animal on his or her board covers it up. Repeat until all the pictures have been matched.

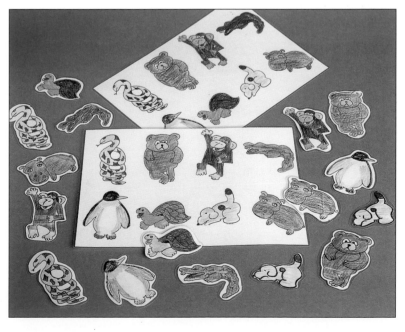

Mathematics

- Use the Spot display and ask the children to count the number of animals in the story. Let them put the animals in order, for example 'Sally found the bear first, the snake second ... '.

- Make a 'Spot game' by drawing the outline of Spot on card and having a collection of spots to place on his body. Use a die with one or two spots on each of its faces and take turns to throw the die and add the right number of spots to his body.

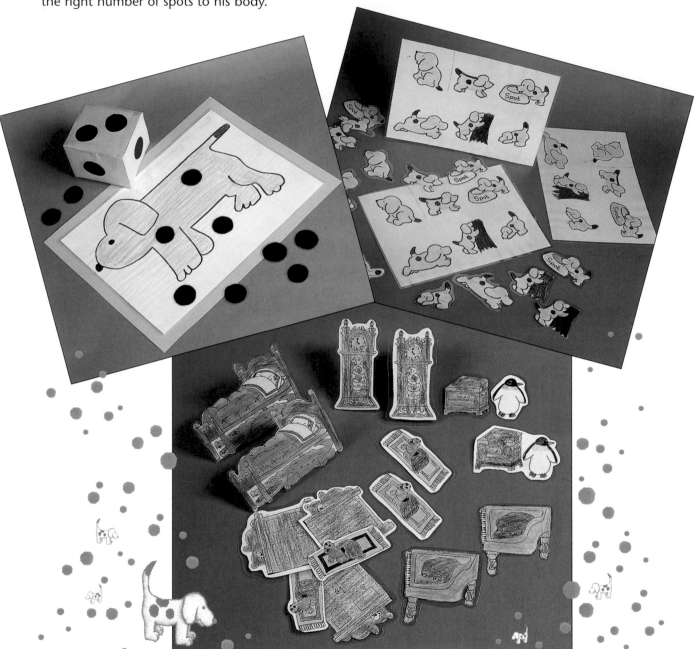

- Play a matching game. Make a set of boards showing Spot in different positions. Match the cut-out pictures of Spot with the same pictures on the board.

- Provide pairs of cards showing the animals hiding amongst the furniture, as described in the story. Encourage the children to match the pairs of cards while emphasising the positional language, such as 'under', 'behind' and 'near to'.

- Provide a bag of differently shaped biscuits and some sorting trays or hoops. Ask the children to sort the biscuits into sets according to their shapes.

Sand and Water

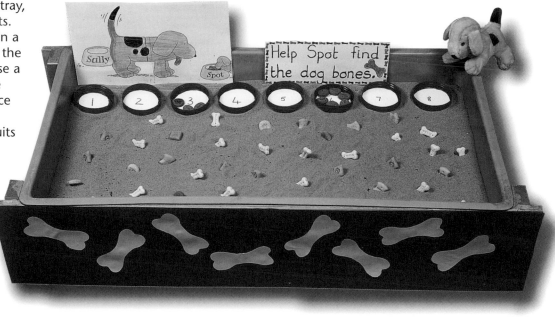

- In the dry sand tray, bury dog biscuits. Write numbers in a row of bowls in the tray. Children use a sieve to find the biscuits and place the appropriate number of biscuits in each bowl.

- Freeze large containers of water to make icebergs. Place in the water tray with white net curtains to represent snow, and different sized penguins. Discuss where penguins live. Use for imaginative play.

- Create a swamp in the jungle by using large sods of long grass, pebbles, logs of wood and potted plants. Hide toy snakes and crocodiles amongst the grass. Discuss where these creatures live. Encourage the children to use the scene for imaginative play.

Our World

- Use a range of reclaimed materials to make the places where Sally looked for Spot, for example: grandfather clock, wardrobe and basket. Provide a wide variety of materials for joining and fastening, such as sticky tape, string, paper clips, glue and split pins. Encourage the children to select the materials themselves.

- Discuss what the wardrobe, the clock, the piano and the box are used for.

- Discuss the places where Sally looked for Spot (the wardrobe, the clock, the piano and the box). Ask: 'In which rooms do you think she looked?' 'Where was the clock?' 'Where was the wardrobe?' As a group, draw a plan of the house and the route Sally took to find Spot.

Creative Work

- Let the children help to make a large grandfather clock and wardrobe from boxes. Paint the items and place in the home corner for children to use in role-play.

- Encourage children to mix their own colours. Arrange items beside an easel, left to right in the following order: water, sponge, powder paint (in small containers), small palette. Children dip their brush into the water, onto the sponge, into the paint and mix it in the small palette, and then paint onto the paper. Encourage this method when painting characters from the story.

- Look closely at the Spot toy dog and draw from observation (see photographs on page 47). Talk through the details on the dog – where the ears are, the spots on the body, the tongue, the eyes and the tail.

- Encourage the children to follow a simple recipe card to make their own salt dough. The recipe card should include the following: 1 cup of flour, $\frac{1}{2}$ cup of salt, 1 teaspoon of oil, 4 tablespoons (approximately) of water. Mix the ingredients together. Colour some dough green and some yellow, then use to model animals from the story. Place on a greased baking tray and bake in a pre-heated oven at 120°C (250°F, gas mark 3) until firm. Varnish, if desired.

⚠ **Note:** Ensure that children are supervised if they are present during the baking.

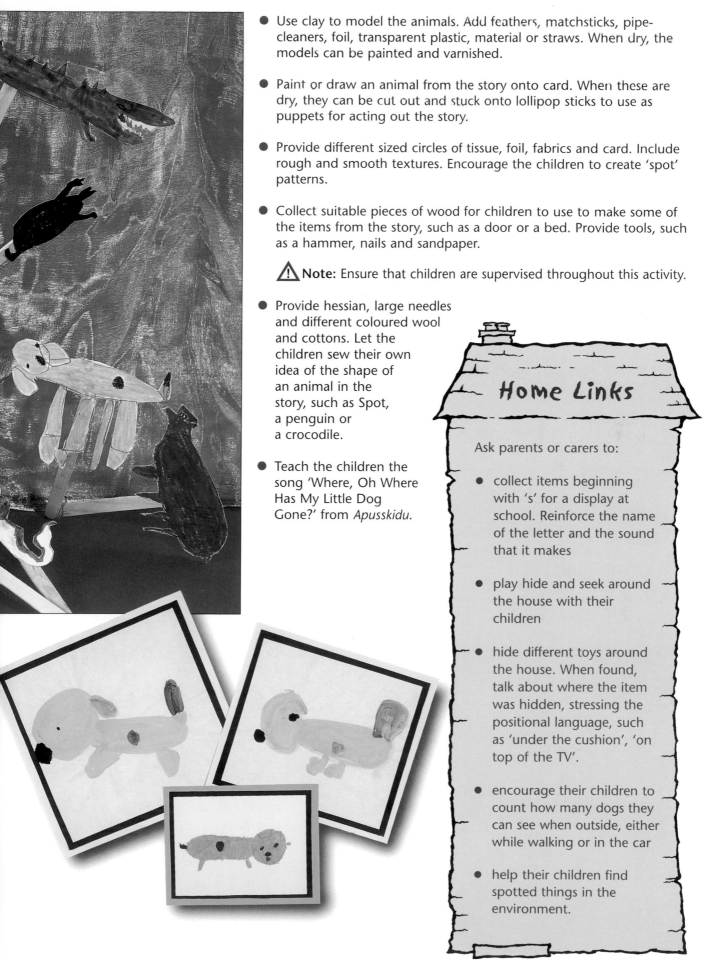

- Use clay to model the animals. Add feathers, matchsticks, pipe-cleaners, foil, transparent plastic, material or straws. When dry, the models can be painted and varnished.

- Paint or draw an animal from the story onto card. When these are dry, they can be cut out and stuck onto lollipop sticks to use as puppets for acting out the story.

- Provide different sized circles of tissue, foil, fabrics and card. Include rough and smooth textures. Encourage the children to create 'spot' patterns.

- Collect suitable pieces of wood for children to use to make some of the items from the story, such as a door or a bed. Provide tools, such as a hammer, nails and sandpaper.

⚠ **Note:** Ensure that children are supervised throughout this activity.

- Provide hessian, large needles and different coloured wool and cottons. Let the children sew their own idea of the shape of an animal in the story, such as Spot, a penguin or a crocodile.

- Teach the children the song 'Where, Oh Where Has My Little Dog Gone?' from *Apusskidu*.

Home Links

Ask parents or carers to:

- collect items beginning with 's' for a display at school. Reinforce the name of the letter and the sound that it makes

- play hide and seek around the house with their children

- hide different toys around the house. When found, talk about where the item was hidden, stressing the positional language, such as 'under the cushion', 'on top of the TV'.

- encourage their children to count how many dogs they can see when outside, either while walking or in the car

- help their children find spotted things in the environment.

Mrs Mopple's Washing Line

Learning Intentions

- To develop the imagination. To introduce the difference between capital and lower-case letters.

- To recognise and order numbers from 1–10. To become familiar with pairs. To use rhymes and songs for simple subtraction.

- To develop children's knowledge and understanding of the weather. To introduce the concept of simple evaporation by drying clothes.

- To develop children's observational skills. To enjoy and memorise songs. To listen to music and respond to it.

Starting Points

- Make a display of the characters from the story *Mrs Mopple's Washing Line* by Anita Hewett. Check that the children know the names of the farm animals (pig, turkey, chicken, cow and rabbit). Also in the display, include a pair of white gloves, a pair of black-and-white striped socks, a pink petticoat and a red spotted handkerchief.

- Show the cover of the book to the children and ask them what the lady is doing and what they think the story is about. Read the story and introduce the characters one by one from the display.

Language and Literacy

- Make the home corner into Mrs Mopple's kitchen. Erect a clothes line and provide a bowl and pegs, along with socks, gloves, a petticoat and a handkerchief for the children to wash. If possible, use water to wash the clothes. Place dressing-up clothes and animal masks in the home corner for the children to act out the story.

- Make books in the shape of a sock, a petticoat or a spotted handkerchief (see photograph on page 48). Ask children to retell the story in pictures and writing.

- Make up a different ending to the story.

- Sequence the story using a flannel board and pictures from the story.

- While reading the story, point out the letter 'm' in 'Mrs', 'Mopple', 'Monday' and 'measles'. Explain the difference between the capital 'M' in the names and the lower-case 'm'. Play 'I Spy', using words beginning with 'm'.

- Discuss with the children what they thought Mrs Mopple was making for dinner. Make a list as the children suggest items.

- Play a memory game, 'I did the washing and washed …'. Encourage the children to repeat what was said previously and to add their own ideas. Use props to help if necessary.

- Make a lotto game and tape the sounds of the animals from the story. Encourage the children to listen carefully.

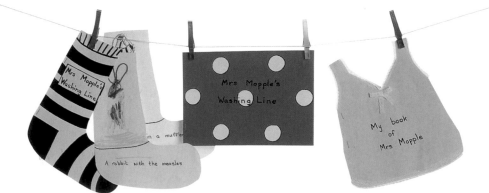

Mathematics

- Encourage the children to sort a collection of farm animals into numbered sets of 1–5 or 1–10, as appropriate. Introduce the following vocabulary: 'count', 'match', 'more than', 'less than', 'sort into sets'.

- Help the children to count how many animals there are in the story. Teach them number rhymes and songs with 'five' in them. For example:

> Five little hats so bright and gay
> Were dancing around on a line one day
> Along came the wind, blowing through the town,
> And one little hat came tumbling down.

Repeat the verse with 4, 3, 2 and 1, and for different items of clothing. Encourage the children to act out the rhymes. Allow one child to count the number of children left at the end of each verse before continuing.

- Make a collection of gloves, socks and shoes, and encourage the children to match the pairs. Emphasise the word 'pair' and demonstrate that it means two.

- Use the items of clothing in the display and ask the children to put them in the right order. What is washed and pegged out on the line first? What is washed and pegged out second? Repeat with the animals from the display. Which animal came first?

- Erect a clothes line in the mathematics area. Fill a small basket with the outlines of clothes cut out from card and number the card clothes 1–10. Pin matching numbered shapes in order on the wall behind the clothes line. Encourage the children to match the numbers and put them in the correct order, or to state which one is missing when one is removed.

Sand and Water

- Use farm animals, play people, small wooden bricks and greenery to make a farm in dry sand. Encourage the children to make pens for each set of animals and use these for imaginative play and language development.

- In the water tray, use different types of washing materials each day to wash Mrs Mopple's clothes. Use hard soap, flakes, soap powder, washing-up liquid and shampoo. Hang up the clothes to dry.

Our World

- If possible, take the children on a visit to a farm. Make a book of the photographs taken to record the visit, writing a sentence under each photograph and let the children use it as a reading book about their farm visit.

- Show the children a selection of vegetables (raw carrots, onions, cabbage and potatoes) and discuss how they grow. Help the children to slice the vegetables and then place them in a bowl with water and a stock cube. Cook in the microwave to make vegetable soup. Talk about how the vegetables have changed now they are cooked. Let the children taste the soup.

- Drip paint or food colouring onto pieces of wet fabric. Ask the children to look closely at how it spreads and the change that takes place as it dries.

- After washing clothes in the home corner or water tray, place them outside on a washing line during different weather. Check and discuss how the clothes dry.

Creative Work

- Paint the characters in the story. Encourage the children to mix their own powder paint in a palette. Let them add collage material to their paintings to represent the clothes the animals wore.

- Paint pictures of a farmyard. Provide a range of materials for children to add to their paintings and make into collages.

- Make a tape of different pieces of music that represent different types of weather. Encourage the children to listen to each piece and state what kind of weather it reminds them of. Let them move to the music.

Home Links

Ask parents or carers to:

- collect objects beginning with 'm' for their children to bring into school for a display

- let their children sort the washing into sets and find the biggest sock, the smallest sock, etc.

- let their children wash some small items of clothing, using soap powder or a bar of soap and hang them out to dry

- watch a weather report on television with their children, and talk about the weather each day.

Peace at Last

Learning Intentions

- To be aware of the different feelings of the characters in the story. To recall the story.

- To know the language of size and use it correctly (tall, taller, tallest; small, smaller, smallest, etc.).

- To know the differences between night and day and to know what can be seen at night that is not generally seen during the day.

- To be aware of different sounds and be able to produce them using musical instruments. To print using a variety of materials and equipment.

Starting Points

- Read the story *Peace at Last* by Jill Murphy, using props in the story box (three differently sized bears, a cuckoo clock, an owl, a hedgehog, a cat, a bird and an alarm clock).

- Ask the children if there has been a time when they could not sleep. Why couldn't they sleep? What did they do? Ask the children to share some of their experiences.

Language and Literacy

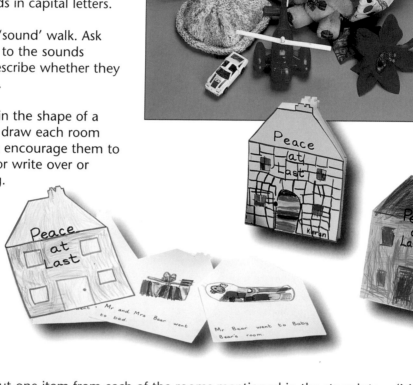

- Encourage the children to use the props to retell the story in their own words. Act out the story as a group activity.

- Reread the story to a small group. Point out the words that are in capital letters, explaining that they are in capitals so that we say them loudly. Encourage the children to join in with the words in capital letters.

- Take the children on a 'sound' walk. Ask them to listen carefully to the sounds around them and to describe whether they are loud or soft sounds.

- Make individual books in the shape of a house. Let the children draw each room with Mr Bear in it, then encourage them to write their own words or write over or under an adult's writing.

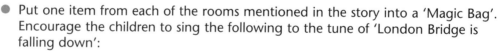

- Put one item from each of the rooms mentioned in the story into a 'Magic Bag'. Encourage the children to sing the following to the tune of 'London Bridge is falling down':

  What is in the magic bag, magic bag, magic bag?
  What is in the magic bag? What can you feel?'

  Ask the children to feel an item in the Magic Bag. Encourage them to describe it so that the other children can guess what it is and identify the room it is associated with in the story.

- Make up a different ending for the story and draw a picture to depict the new ending.

- Ask individual children to sit on the carpet and use their imagination to decide where Mr Bear could go to get some sleep. Write down the places the children suggest and help them to draw a picture of where Mr Bear could go. Mount the drawings and descriptions on carpet-shaped cards. Combine the children's work to create a display.

- Name all the sounds that Mr Bear hears. Make a collection of the items and label them with the name and the sound that they make. Make a game of matching the sound with the correct item.

Mathematics

- Use toy bears of different sizes and let the children put the bears in order of size from the largest to the smallest, then the smallest to the largest.

- Compare the sizes of the bears. Ask the children to think of different words to describe the size of the bears, for example 'small', 'tiny', 'little'. Emphasise the language of size, such as 'middle-sized', 'medium-sized', 'in-between'; 'large', 'huge', 'gigantic'; 'big', 'bigger', 'biggest'.

- Describe where Mr Bear went 1st, 2nd, 3rd, and so on.

- Provide a small, brick-built bed and some differently sized bears. How many bears will fit onto the bed? Let the children estimate first and then self-test.

- Weigh bears of different sizes against non-standard measures, such as a shoe or construction cubes.

- Play the 'Honey Pot Game'. Make a straight track for six bears and divide each track into sections. Place a pot of honey at the end of each track. Put the colours of the bears on two dice. Each child throws the dice in turn and moves the appropriate bears along the track. The first bear to reach their honey pot is the winner.

Our World

- As you read the story, talk about the differences between night and day. Ask the children what they might see at night that they don't see during the day (moon, stars, owls, bats, hedgehogs). Make a chart, entitled 'We see these at night'.

- Discuss what Mr Bear might have had to eat when he went into the kitchen. Make a list on a large piece of paper or a whiteboard of what he would need. During the week, let the children make toast and choose what to put on it – marmalade, jam, honey or lemon curd.

- Use reclaimed materials to make the sink, clock and refrigerator in the story. Cover with white paper and place in the home corner. Label them with sounds from the story.

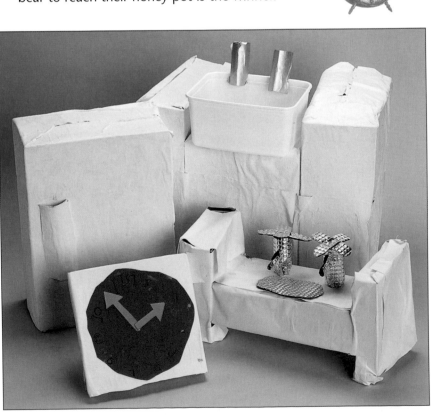

Sand and Water

● Half-fill some containers with water and place them in the water tray. Ask the children to estimate how many bears will fit into the container to make the water rise to the top. Test out their theory. Ask them what they think will happen if the container is full of water before the bears are put in.

Creative Work

● Paint or draw a picture of one of the bears or a favourite part of the story.

● Use handprints to make pictures of the owl and the hedgehog.

● Make a display of the musical instruments that the children can use to accompany the sounds in the story as it is read.

● Make patterned bedcovers for the bear's bed out of a range of materials.

● Print borders for baby bear's bedroom. Use repeating patterns of teddies and aeroplanes.

Home Links

Ask parents or carers to:

● talk about the differences between night and day and to point out the moon and stars when their children are going to bed

● encourage their children to listen to the sounds around them (the swish of passing cars, the drone of the refrigerator, the hum of the computer)

● let their children draw round cutters or templates of stars, circles, moons, etc. Colour in the shapes and cut them out. Make wallpaper by sticking them onto sheets of paper.

A Dragon in a Wagon

Learning Intentions

- To reread a text with patterns of rhyme and detect rhymes in stories and nursery rhymes. To use knowledge of rhymes to find rhyming words.

- To compare sizes of creatures in the story.

- To know about different habitats and appreciate the different parts of the world where animals live.

- To use control technology.

- To weave and use wire and papier-mâché to create creatures in the story. To draw and paint individual representations of the story.

Starting Points

- Introduce the book *A Dragon in a Wagon* by Lynley Dodd to the children. Talk about the front cover and point out the name of the author and the illustrator. Ask the children: 'What do you think the story will be about?'

- Read the story. Draw attention to the rhymes in the story, especially the rhyming pairs on each page. Encourage the children to raise their hand whenever they hear words that rhyme.

Language and Literacy

- Use other stories, such as *Slinki Malinki, Open the Door* by Lynley Dodd; *Don't Put Your Finger in the Jelly, Nelly!* by Nick Sharratt; and *Don't Forget the Bacon* by Pat Hutchins. Pause before the rhyming word is read out to encourage the children to predict it.

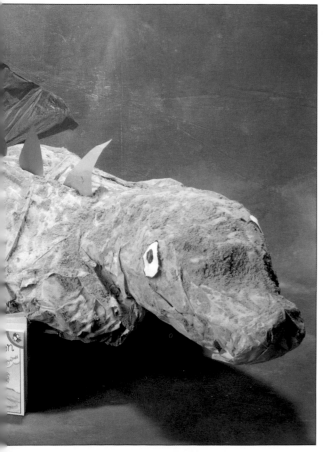

- Teach the children nursery rhymes such as 'Hickory, dickory dock', 'Old Mother Hubbard' and 'Twinkle, twinkle, little star'. Encourage them to think of alternative rhyming words for the rhymes.

- Provide a selection of objects and make sure that the children can identify them. Ask them to match objects according to their rhyme, for example 'pear' with 'chair', and 'sock' with 'lock'. (See photograph on page 56.)

- Provide a selection of mounted, laminated pictures. Ask the children to match an object to a picture that rhymes with it, for example they could place a rope on a picture of some soap.

- Play games in which the children find the rhymes.

- Encourage the children to draw pictures from the story that represent rhyming pairs. Use them to make a big book.

- Create an interesting and exciting book area with children's representations of the rhymes in the story.

- Play ring games to reinforce rhyming patterns, for example 'Ring-a-ring-a-roses'.

Mathematics

● Compare the sizes of creatures in the book. Use mathematical vocabulary (such as 'big', 'small', 'large', 'tiny', 'huge', 'biggest', 'smallest, 'middle-sized').

● When constructing a giraffe to place in a part of the room (see Creative Work), measure the height required using non-standard measures, such as hands, cubes and string.

● When making the wagon for the dragon (see Creative Work), let the children measure the wood using their hands so that the wagon is big enough for the dragon to fit into.

● Look at the patterns on the snake and the giraffe. Let the children construct their own patterns using coloured pegs, cotton reels or beads.

Our World

● Discuss with the children the different parts of the world where the creatures live. Talk about the different habitats and discuss the differences between where the bat, snake, whale and giraffe live. Encourage the children to create appropriate landscapes in which to fit the animals.

● Talk about animals that live in the wild and how some are captured and placed in a zoo. Talk about the preservation of endangered species and conservation issues. Ask the children what they think.

● Compare imaginary and fictitious animals or creatures, such as dragons, unicorns, monsters and giants, with familiar animals and people.

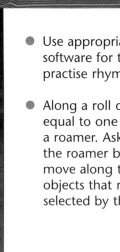

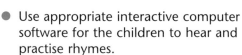

● Use appropriate interactive computer software for the children to hear and practise rhymes.

● Along a roll of paper, mark divisions equal to one unit of movement for a roamer. Ask the children to control the roamer by programming it to move along the roll of paper to objects that rhyme with an object selected by the child.

Creative Work

- Use wire and papier-mâché to mould and create a dragon. Encourage the children to look at the picture in the book and mix the correct colour to paint it. Add sand to paint to create a textured, scaly effect.

- Provide a selection of wood and a range of tools for children to make the dragon's wagon. Display the story book nearby and encourage the children to look at the shape of the wagon.

  ⚠ **Note:** Ensure that children are supervised throughout this activity.

- Use withies, cylinders and paper to build a tall giraffe. Encourage the children to look closely at the patterns on a giraffe's back and select appropriate coloured paper to represent them.

- Provide a selection of materials, such as coloured paper, wool and fabric, for the children to cut into strips and weave into a scarf.

- Encourage the children to paint and/or make a collage of their favourite rhyme in the story. Display with appropriate labels for the children to read.

- Teach the children the song 'A Dragon Went Over the Mountain' to the tune 'The Bear Went Over the Mountain' from *Apusskidu*. Encourage the children to choose instruments to accompany the singing.

- Choose different extracts of music to represent animal movements, such as *Carnival of the Animals* by Saint-Saëns, *Noye's Fludde* by Britten and *Peter and the Wolf* by Prokofiev. Encourage the children to move and respond to the music.

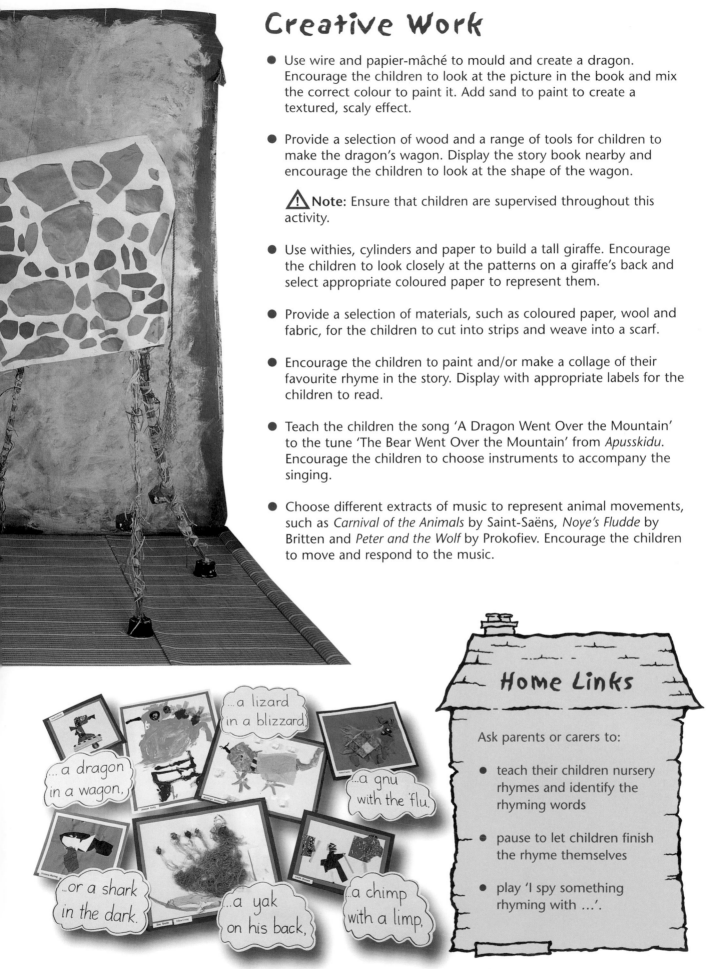

...a lizard in a blizzard,

...a dragon in a wagon,

...a gnu with the 'flu,

...or a shark in the dark.

...a yak on his back,

...a chimp with a limp,

Home Links

Ask parents or carers to:

- teach their children nursery rhymes and identify the rhyming words

- pause to let children finish the rhyme themselves

- play 'I spy something rhyming with ...'.

59

Jasper's Beanstalk

Learning Intentions

- To encourage children to use their imaginations by changing the ending of the story. To act out the story. To learn the days of the week.

- To match, sort and count beans. To record the growth of a bean.

- To know the names and purposes of gardening tools. To know that plants need air, light and water to grow.

- To respond to the story through a variety of materials.

Opening times
9.30 – 10.30
1.30 – 2.30

open

Please take a basket.

flowers 1p each

flowers

plants 5p

plants

Scartho Garden Cer

plant pot

5p

JASPER'S BEANSTALK

Starting Points

- Introduce the book *Jasper's Beanstalk* by Nick Butterworth and Mick Inkpen. Look at the cover of the book and discuss the colours used in the title.

- Name the garden tools that Jasper is holding.

- Read the story using the story box to hold some of the props.

Language and Literacy

- Recall the sequence of the story with the children. Provide the book, a toy cat, mini-insects, tools and a wheelbarrow. Encourage the children to act out the story individually or with others.

- Ask the children how the story can be developed. What happens to the beanstalk? Does Jasper climb it? If so, where does he go? What happens to him? Act out a few suggestions.

- Create a garden centre in the home corner. Include a cash register, pots, Wellington boots, flowers, plants in pots, tools, telephone, telephone directory, advertisements and notices, such as 'open' and 'closed'. Children act out the roles of customers and shopkeepers.

- Display gardening tools and some growing plants (see Our World, page 63). Label them with pictures and words. Ask the children to find the label that says, for example, 'cress' and 'beans'.

- Draw simple outline pictures showing the growth of a plant. Ask the children to place them in sequence and to write their own story about the plant, by using their own symbols or by copying an adult's writing.

- Make labels for the days of the week, display them and let the children sequence them. Make a game of finding the correct day for when Jasper watered the bean, and so on.

- As a group, make a big book about Jasper. Display it in the book corner so that the children can read it.

- Take photographs of the children acting out the story. Make a book and write a simple sentence under each photograph, such as 'We play in the garden centre', 'We can act', 'We plant beans'.

- Use the children's paintings to create a story board with sentences displayed to encourage them to read the story.

Mathematics

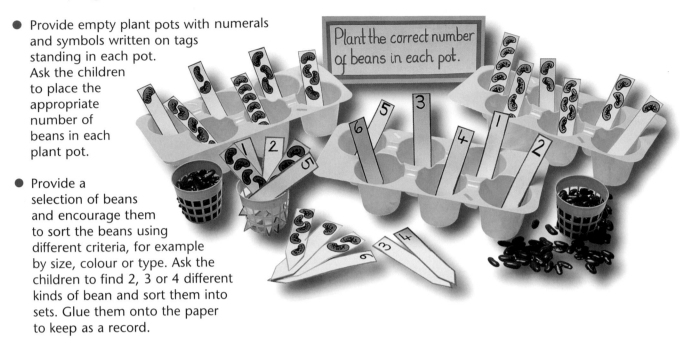

Plant the correct number of beans in each pot.

- Provide empty plant pots with numerals and symbols written on tags standing in each pot. Ask the children to place the appropriate number of beans in each plant pot.

- Provide a selection of beans and encourage them to sort the beans using different criteria, for example by size, colour or type. Ask the children to find 2, 3 or 4 different kinds of bean and sort them into sets. Glue them onto the paper to keep as a record.

- Plant some beans and record their growth. Measure the height of their growth using construction cubes. Record in individual books.

- Provide a variety of differently sized plant pots. Ask the children to sort them into sets of the same size and then order them sequentially, from smallest to largest and then largest to smallest.

This week we are looking at how beans grow.
I have sorted 3 different beans.

This week we are looking at how beans grow.
I have sorted 4 different beans.

This week we are looking at how beans grow.
I have sorted 2 different beans.

Sand and Water

- In wet sand, place small sticks and rakes for the children to make patterns in the sand.

- Put coloured water, watering cans, tubes and funnels in the water tray. Encourage the children to experiment in transferring water from one container to another.

- On a large builder's merchant's tray, place compost, small sand tools and differently sized plant pots. Ask the children to fill the pots and compare sizes, using vocabulary, such as 'full', 'empty', 'half full' and 'half empty' to explain what they are doing. Ask questions such as: 'How many small pots will fill the large pot?'

Our World

- Provide some children's plastic gardening tools and let the children use them in the garden. Discuss their uses and what they are made of.

- Grow broad beans in a cut-down soft-drinks bottle. Line the bottle with one or two dry paper towels or blotting paper. Spoon some sand into the bottom of the container and place the beans down the outside of the paper. Pour water down the side of the bottle to wet the paper and the sand. Encourage the children to predict what they think might happen and talk about conditions for growth (light, water and air). Observe the beans every day.

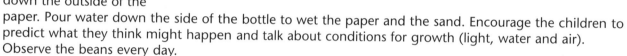

- Discuss what are good conditions for growth. Investigate what happens to beans or seeds grown with and without water, and with and without light.

- Cut the tops off carrots and place them on saucers. Water only one, then place them all on the investigation table. Observe and record.

- Place white carnations and celery in pots of water and add dye to the water. Ask the children to predict what will happen. Observe each day and notice the differences. Draw the results.

- Provide a variety of seeds and let the children examine them through a magnifying glass. Plant seeds such as mustard, cress and grass. Talk about the care of plants.

- Take the children outside and look for worms, slugs and snails. Take magnifying glasses to look at them closely. Emphasise the need to handle them gently. Look for similarities and differences.

The following panels appear in the display:

- On Monday Jasper found a bean.
- On Tuesday he planted it.
- On Wednesday he watered it.
- On Thursday he dug and raked and sprayed and hoed it.
- On Saturday he even mowed it!
- On Sunday Jasper waited and waited and waited...
- When Monday came round again he dug it up.
- "That bean will never make a beanstalk", said Jasper.

Jasper's Beanstalk

Now Jasper is looking for Giants!

Creative Work

- Ask the children to choose one part of the story to paint. Display the children's paintings in sequence as a story board with the appropriate sentence written underneath. Use it to ask questions of the children, such as: 'What did Jasper do on Monday?'

- Let the children draw or paint flowers and plants from close observation of the items.

- Make a collection of seed packets. Encourage the children to make their own packets and illustrate the covers.

- Spread glue on a piece of paper and ask the children to make patterns using seeds.

- Use a selection of different materials, such as tissue paper, foil, lace, fabric, twigs, straws and buttons, to make flowers for the 'Garden Centre'.

- Sing action songs such as 'This is the way we plant our seeds' to the tune of 'Here we go round the mulberry bush'.

- Let the children make shakers from plastic cups or cartons, filling each one with a different kind of bean. Ask the children to listen carefully to the different sounds that they make.

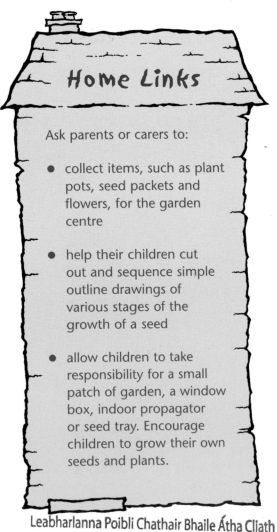

Home Links

Ask parents or carers to:

- collect items, such as plant pots, seed packets and flowers, for the garden centre

- help their children cut out and sequence simple outline drawings of various stages of the growth of a seed

- allow children to take responsibility for a small patch of garden, a window box, indoor propagator or seed tray. Encourage children to grow their own seeds and plants.

Leabharlanna Poibli Chathair Bhaile Átha Cliath
Dublin City Public Libraries